KAMA SUTRA

© Rupa Classic India Series 1993
First published 1993 by Rupa & Co.
7/16 Ansari Road, Daryaganj, New Delhi 110 002
Thirteenth impression 1999
Set in 9.6 on 12 Palatino by Megatechnics, New Delhi
Printed in India by Gopsons Papers Ltd., Noida.

ISBN 81-7167-160-8

Design : Pankaj Goel
General Editor : Amrita Kumar

KAMA SUTRA

Rupa & Co

INTRODUCTION

Few books on the subject of sex are as open and sincere as the Kama Sutra. But more than a sex manual, it is an essay on sexual etiquette in the context of the Hindu attitude to social behaviour. It includes a discussion of subjects such as the education of women, freedom of social intercourse and the remarriage of widows. In reflecting a condition of high civilization in ancient India, it exposes modern societies as comparatively guilt-ridden and oppressed. Most remarkable is that in discussing the various phases of love making, it treats the male and the female as equal partners. All other ancient treatises on love look at women as of a lower order, as creatures created by God solely for the pleasure of man.

The Kama Sutra was written some time between the first and the fourth centuries A.D. Its author is Vatsyayana, who compiled his treatise from the writings of various sages while a student of religion in Benaras. Originally in Sanskrit, the English translation brought the Kama Sutra worldwide recognition as the greatest book on love ever written.

In the following pages the part of the Kama Sutra devoted to the sexual union is presented through paintings from various schools of Indian art. It is suggested to the reader to remember that they are as much an expression of longing for primordial unity as of sexual passion.

4

Women being of a tender nature, want tender beginnings, and when they are forcibly approached by men with whom they are but slightly acquainted, they sometimes suddenly become haters of sexual connection, and sometimes even haters of the male sex.

At the first time of sexual union the passion of the male is intense, and his time is short, but in subsequent unions on the same day the reverse of this is the case.

With the female, however, it is the contrary, for at the
first time her passion is weak, and then her time long,
but on subsequent occasions on the same day, her
passion is intense and her time short, until her passion
is satisfied.

When a man bites a woman forcibly, she should angrily do the same to him with double force. Thus if men and women act according to each other's liking, their love for each other will not be lessened even in one hundred years.

8

When love becomes intense, pressing with the nails or scratching the body with them is practised.

When a curved mark is made on the breast by means of the five nails, it is called a peacock's foot.

When five marks with the nails are made close to one another near the nipple of the breast, it is called the jump of a hare.

When a person is going on a journey, and makes a mark on the thighs or on the breast, it is called a token *of remembrance. On such an occasion three or four lines are impressed close to one another with the nails.*

*When the yoni is lowered, and the upper part of it is
struck with the lingam, it is called* piercing.

When the same thing is done on the lower part of the yoni, it is called rubbing.

When both sides of the yoni are rubbed in this way, it is called the blow of a bull.

When the legs are contracted, and thus held by the lover before his bosom, it is called the pressed position.

Right : When only one of her legs is stretched out, it is called the half pressed position.

When one of her legs is placed on the head, and the other is stretched out, it is called the fixing of a nail.

Right : *When both the legs of the woman are contracted, and placed on her stomach, it is called the* crab's position.

18

When a man supports himself against a wall, and the woman, sitting on his hands joined together and held underneath her, throws her arms round his neck, and putting her thighs alongside his waist, moves herself by her feet, which are touching the wall against which the man is leaning, it is called the suspended congress.

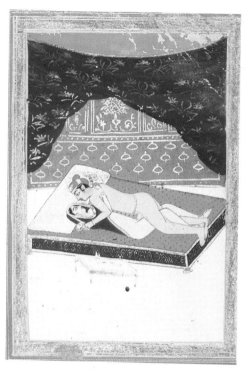

When the legs of both the male and the female are stretched straight out over each other, it is called the clasping position.

When she raises both of her legs, and places them on her lover's shoulders, it is called the yawning *position.*

When the female raises both of her thighs straight up, it is called the rising *position.*

When the woman places one of her thighs across the thigh of her lover, it is called the twining position.

Right : *When the woman places one of her legs on her lover's shoulder, and stretches the other out, and then places the latter on his shoulder, and stretches out the other and continues to do so alternately, it is called the* splitting of a bamboo.

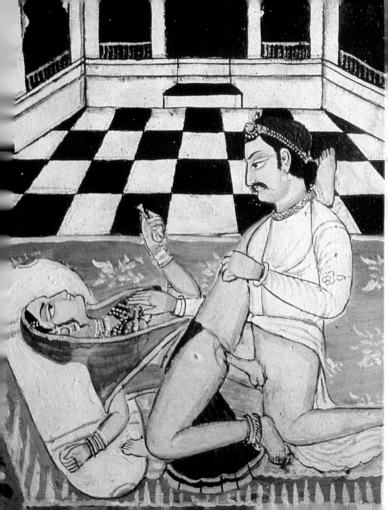

When the thighs are raised and placed one upon the other, it is called the packed position.

When the shanks are placed one upon the other, it is called the lotus-like *position.*

When a woman forcibly holds in her yoni the lingam after it is in, it is called the **mare's** *position.*

When a man and a woman support themselves on each other's bodies, or on a wall, or pillar, and thus while standing engage in congress, it is called supported congress.

When the woman holds the lingam in her yoni, draws it in, presses it, and keeps it thus in her for a long time, it is called a pair of tongs.

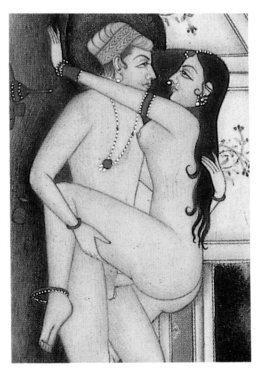

When one of two lovers presses forcibly on one or both
of the thighs of the other between his or her own it is
called the embrace of thighs.

When a woman makes slightly the sounds of singing and cooing, and wishes, as it were, to climb up to him in order to have a kiss, it is called an embrace like the climbing of a tree.

When lovers lie on a bed, and embrace each other
so closely that the arms and thighs of the one are
encircled by the arms and thighs of the other, and are,
as it were, rubbing up against them, this is called an
embrace like the mixture of sesamum seed with rice.

When a man and a woman embrace each other as if they were entering into each other's bodies either while the woman is sitting on the lap of the man, or in front of him, or on a bed, then it is called an embrace like a mixture of milk and water.

34

*When the lingam is removed to some distance from the yoni,
and then forcibly strikes it, it is called* giving a blow.

When, while engaged in congress, she turns round like a wheel, it is called the top.

Right : When, on such an occasion, the man lifts up the middle part of his body, and the woman turns round her middle parts it is called the swing.

When a woman, clinging to a man as a creeper twines round a tree, embraces him, and looks lovingly towards him, it is called an embrace like the twining of a creeper.

When a man places his breast between the breasts of a
woman and presses her with it, it is called the embrace of
the breasts.

When a man presses the jaghana or middle part of the woman's body against his own, and mounts upon her to practice, either scratching with the nail, or finger, or biting, or striking, or kissing, it is called the embrace of the jaghana.

When a man, during congress, turns round, and enjoys the woman without leaving her, while she embraces him round the back all the time, it is called the turning position.

41

When she places her thighs with her legs doubled on them upon her sides, and thus engages in congress, it is called the position of Indrani

Right : *When she lowers her head and raises her middle parts, it is called the* widely opened position.

When the lingam is in the yoni, and moved up and down
frequently, and without being taken out, it is called the
sporting of a sparrow.

When a man and a woman lie down in an inverted order,
i.e., with the head of the one towards the feet of the other and
carry on this congress, it is called the congress of the
crow.

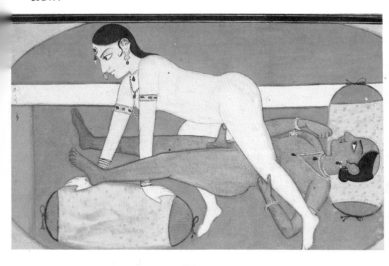

Congress in the anus is called the lower congress.

Right : *When a woman sees that her lover is fatigued by constant congress, she should lay him down upon his back, and give him assistance by acting his part.*

She should get on top of her lover in such a manner as to continue the congress without obstructing the pleasure of it.

She should return his blows and chaffing him, should say, "I was laid down by you, and fatigued with hard congress, I shall now therefore lay you down in return."

49

The rules of the Shastra apply so long as the passion of man is middling, but when the wheel of love is once set in motion, there is then no Shastra and no order.

Even in ordinary things that revolve with great force, such as a potter's wheel, or a top, we find that the motion at first is slow, but by degrees it becomes very rapid.

When a man enjoys two women at the same time, both of whom love him equally, it is called the united congress.

Right : When a man enjoys many women altogether, it is called the congress of a herd of cows.

Many young men enjoy a woman that may be married to one of them, either one after the other, or at the same time. Thus one of them holds her, another enjoys her, a third uses her mouth, a fourth holds her middle part, and in this way they go on enjoying her several parts alternately.

A woman who is very much in love with a man cannot bear to hear the name of her rival mentioned, or to be addressed by her name through mistake. If such takes place, the woman strikes her lover, falls from her bed or

At this time, the lover should attempt to reconcile her with conciliatory words, and should take her up carefully and place her on the bed.

*When she thinks that the conciliatory words and actions of
her lover have reached their utmost, she should then embrace
him, talking to him with harsh and reproachful words, but
at the same time showing a loving desire for congress.*

When one of the two returns from a journey, or is reconciled after having been separated on account of a quarrel, then congress is called the loving congress.

When two persons come together, while their love for each other is still in its infancy, their congress is called the congress of subsequent love.

When a man and a woman come together, though in reality they are both attached to different persons, their congress is then called congress of artificial love.

*When a man, from the beginning to the end of the
congress, though having connection with the woman,
thinks all the time that he is enjoying another one whom
he loves, it is called the* congress of transferred love.

61

Congress between a man and a female water carrier, or a female servant of a caste lower than his own, lasting only until the desire is satisfied, is called congress like that of eunuchs. Here external touches, kisses, and manipulations are not to be employed.

The congress that takes place between two persons who are attached to one another, and which is done according to their own liking is called spontaneous congress.

Love resulting from the constant and continual performance of
some act, is called love acquired by constant practice and habit,
as for instance the love of sexual intercourse, the love of hunting,
the love of drinking, the love of gambling etc.